DRESS WHITES

DRESS WHITES

Poetry

RICHARD GILMORE LOFTUS

ISBN-13: 9781981550180
ISBN-10: 1981550186
Library of Congress Control Number: 2017919033
CreateSpace Independent Publishing Platform
North Charleston, South Carolina

To Sara

It is no use waiting for your ship to come in, unless you have sent one out.

—Belgian proverb

CONTENTS

I

II

I

THE RIVER

Hard, then, I pull the old canoe
across the freshly painted truck
and leave a good long scrape
against the roof,
a pleasure mark,
like bruises
caused by lovers
new to one another's touch.

Today, the river
wears an icy negligee
parted down a dark
and silent middle.
Birds hustle
tree to tree,
and the song of my paddle
swirls underneath.

Afterward, I like
to drive through town,
canoe mounted, bound,
water still clinging to its bow.

AMONG THE SONNETS

At the bookstore
in the discard bin
among the sonnets,
it occurred to me:
I missed her.
Not a longing,
though there was that,
but rather, I did not attend
when there was the chance,
did not chart the freckles of her
arms, shoulders, belly, thighs, and back
whereby I might navigate
those fine shallows, those great depths,
and revisit
her seas and sentiment
now and again.

BUTTERFLY HOUSE

For all we know,
this is the petal,
pooling water,
cleft in the stone
we would come to
on our own.
This air, palpable,
explains these
taut and tapered wings;
and oh, the joy
of take and give,
nectar warming,
a gentle transfer
that loving brings.

You had us
convinced;
it's true.
The rocks,
perfect;
these flowers,
too,
and that distant canopy
of prismed light—
an archetype of ethereal blue.

A world contrived
without chance,
tampered free of incident;
in short, this place,
a paradise.

Our time is quick.
We come; we go.
You win the eyes
but not the soul.

DRESS WHITES

Strange beauty to see
these sails from the shore:
such distant white linens and stays,
luminous in the attending sun,
coming wind,
rising of the day.
No groaning tiller,
aching bow,
quarreling wave
lifting, leveling,
sinking, leavening
the sea for me.
All these, for me
are spread and displayed—
the fall and rise of far-off things,
those that belong to stronger men,
their hammering hearts
and calloused hands
ever on the horizon.

COME HITHER

The water is high, high as ever.
It pushes through grass that borders the sand,
touches intimately all in its press,
steals earth from its bed with moonlight caresses,
begins so sweetly, unveiling its thieving at last.
I understand.
If I were the land,
after swirls so tender and touches forever,
I too might acquiesce, invite the wet to
flow, overwhelm, in the end, take me home.
You and I, water and sand, this
scrimmage—delight and deluge, threat and refuge,
with stars as witness, the moon as mistress:
a testament, for all we know.

PYGMALION

The dust has settled.
The pallet served us well.
A full moon slips
through the workshop window,
arrays the array of
hammers and chisels,
casts cool light
on our bed.
I study the marble
of your breast—
the vein, just so,
rising, falling
as it should;
the dimples
at your hip and chin;
your lips;
and lustrous eyes
that invite
a lover
to love
his own reflection.

And yet
I think to myself,
I can do better than this.

MINOTAUR

Beneath the cellar door,
you know he's there.
Down winding stairs
and corridors of broken chairs,
beyond the derelict washer, dryer,
scrub sink, and rusted Flexible Flyer,
you know he's there—

propped on elbow,
jug at hand,
his broad, hairy chest
heaving slow, at rest,
alert to nothing
but the lifted latch
at the top of the stairs.

PLANNING THE GARDEN

Like the photo of a mail-order bride,
the seed catalog describes
what will be needed
in the ensuing weeks:
a fit and proper bed
laid out east to west,
a vessel of tendered water,
a strong sun to part the veil of trees.
With this,
they will rise,
bloom,
thrive,
and then recline
in autumn.
A lesson in love.
A lesson in kind.
Seeds arcing from my hand
before the package has arrived.

SPANISH IS A LOVING TONGUE

En français,
la roche leans into la mer,
rock, strong, steady,
against a rising
wave and tide
that takes in whispered crevices,
all stones before her glide.

Italiano
wants less to separate
loving "this" from stalwart "that":
il poeta—man, masculine—
untroubled by his feminine end,
spills ink on parchment,
his oceans mixed with land.

But English—O rock, O water,
sounds to cheat the tongue
of caresses it might summon
below, beside, above.
So we steal cabaña
from the Spanish,
kneel in slatted light
to spy in wordless wonder
and please our voyeur's eye.

JAZZ

At loving last, maybe, I get it.

After
spritzes of cologne and perfume
and phantom sounds in another room,
an echoing face in the windowpane,
tongue-tipped taste of gin and vermouth,
and the stroking fingers in memory

come
the smell of neck, belly, and hips;
the parting sound of arriving lips;
filament hair clinging to sweat;
the salt gathered wet beneath your breast;
the clasp of my hand holding your wrist:

a ready mix
of want and do,
lingering horns
in a steady groove,
a beautiful beating
that drums the truth.

GROUNDSKEEPER

If I judge love
by the romping, the rude, the many
calling from the bleacher pews,
I never would have reached for you.
They know their lime and lines, all right,
names, numbers,
and programs—
but I know you.
I know each blade of you,
pressed and risen
in morning mist, in twilight;
know the sun that travels you,
direct, oblique, in between,
to give you color while cheers surround you.
But I know too the separate night,
how the moon combs you gray and blue,
awakens the silvery spread of you,
and leaves you waiting for me.

SPARROW

It was her moment,
but I took it for my own.
Through the storm window,
I felt the pressing cold.
She was at the feeder
warmed alone
by the fall and rise
of her brown-plumed breast.

Approached,
she turned her eye
but did not have the strength or fear
to lift her wings.
I heaped seeds around
her clutching feet. Absurdly,
you might think.
But there was an appointment. In town.
And so I left
the world wavering in her tiny oval eye,
an eye the size
of a lone husked seed.

Who's to say how it ended that night?
Clinging to that perch
until the slightest wind toppled her.
Perhaps one more flight,
her wings astonished by the thickness of the sky.

On my return
I had to park the car,
check the lights,
fiddle with the garage door
before looking for the bird.
I found her in the snow.
In my gloved hand
I raised her up,
her prescient eye still
turned toward mine,
her silent mouth
singing to my bones.

BONFIRE

In now from the fire outside,
I search the books
for Robert Frost.
This time is his and mine.
I turn the pages—"Birch Swinger,"
leaping, bending, tree to tree—
and note among the words and lines
the smudged place
from a fire gone by
that tells my favoring of these favorite lines.
Like the bare skin of a collier's wife,
they show the reader's loving mark.
I'm thinking now of hips and breasts,
a contour map of desire:
fingertips that smudge her gray
with coal caresses by candlelight.
Here, on this page,
I find the mark,
my collier self,
again today—
a love of fire
in autumn time,
the flame, the heat,
the smoke and soot,
the turning leaves of poetry.

WINTER

We listened to a lost ship in the harbor;
we listened to the train that knew its way,
counted each remaining stubborn leaf,
watched the curling smoke gather by the bay,
recalled the many times we played this game:
I, dead to his prowling breath;
he, circling my December bed,
daring me to make my move—
reach for a cigarette,
reach for a beer, or better yet,
return his gray-eyed, insolent stare.
We listened to his lean heart tick
the calendar of days,
until, at last,
he decided, he alone,
it was time to leave;
sniffed my face, the bed,
the corners of the room;
followed his own soft tread
down the hall, to the yard,
across town, fields, continents,
returning, as ever,
with each departing step.

HOUDINI

The knot is never the same,
nor the coiled rope,
clasp of the lock,
hold of the box.
Different, too,
each silent fall,
slam of water,
weight of the sea.
It never is quite the same, you see.
I, too, am changed,
wriggling, still,
lean or fat,
twisted, straight,
altered by descent and ascent,
fallen and raised,
fat head singing,
"Escape…escape,"
as I slip the knot,
shed the coil,
trip the lock,
erupt from the box,
from the sea,
to the air,
to the sun,
to the cry of the crowd,
to me…

with a drum in my chest
to number the days
till it beats, once again,
in the sea.

THE SUMMER SHED

Here is the rusty pail
seen through a broken pane.
The ax handle
has lost its blade—
evidence
of those who stayed,
who scraped and painted
wooden boats,
kept memory alive
on laundry lines
in calico.
Rear guard,
adversarial,
however phrased,
with a god
who will not reason
with our days:
they kept history's loss at bay,
kept a shelf of porcelain
that would perish
by accident
inevitably one day
yet assures us all of
our intent to stay.

BULL DANCER OF CRETE

You come for
the plait of my hair,
my small lifted bosom,
still-boyish hips,
flounced fallen skirt as
it greets the sand,
the trim of my thighs
and dark-olive skin,
but I—
I have come for the bull.
And he has come for me.

You come for
the blood of my skull,
the rake of my back,
my torn, broken breast,
the twisted wreck
of what's left
crushed in the dirt,
but I—
I have come for the bull.
And he has come for me.

I have come
like the scent of the sea
in my hair,
in my skin,

the sea that moves through me
buoyant, salt wet,
above sand
above you
and for one moment fast,
the quick black back
and horns of this creature
that hurtles toward me.

And you,
in your fat,
your stall,
with grease-covered lips
can call and curse
and jaw and jeer;
you, who leave when it's done
for home, arm in arm—

as I vault through the air
and my hands touch his back,
as my feet leave the ground
and dance on the sun,
as the earth is my sky
and the sky is my ground

—you will want one thing.
You will want to be me.

DOGGEREL

He moves,
as I do,
crudely through the house
sniffing, sniffing
cupboards, countertops;
consoled by treats, drinks,
the swinging cool
of the Frigidaire
that soothes the profanity
of his thinking.
Thus we spend our vapid hours,
until at last it's time
to rend once-living things
for the pleasure of our bowels.
We eat, we nap, we wander—
boxed animals that we are,
we nose the blinds apart
to watch the other animals glide by,
jealous of their asphalt trysts,
coveting their treats and drinks,
their Frigidaires,
the profanity of their thinking.
And thus we spend
our morning, afternoon, and evening,
await each night's

duvet and ceiling,
cool and moonless
though they may be.
We burrow, like lovers,
curved in concert to a single dream,
safe from the world—
the world safe from him and me.

READING MARY OLIVER

The fire has taken at last,
as have the lines from
this far-off woman's poetry.

Her hummingbirds are not mine,
nor the necklace stiles
of her countryside.

The turn of her words
fetches a softer cheek.
The hand she holds is mild.

But look here—
the common seagull cry,
a wind to rile a New England beach,

words that murmur
through a harp in the reeds.
These, too, are mine.

I take a rough tool
from the rack
and tumble coals,
glowing
with the promise of heat.

WAITING FOR ORION

An October sky—
a lattice
of ink and light
folded over and over
upon itself—
mingled specks of heads and limbs,
swords and centaurs,
each
a sphinx
of borrowed parts and pieces.
They are lost to my untutored eye,
an eye
that fails to find a point of purchase,
to shape these lights to a schoolbook paradigm.
So it is, with stars I wait,
attending to the eastern sky
where two months on
the hunter comes,
all tunic
and sword about to strike,
and by his light
set each star in place,
lend names and reason to the December night.
This hunter from the eastern sky
will take us to the prey.

BALTHUS AT DUSK

A hundred steps from my park bench,
she comes running.
To me. To me. To me. I think.
Polite, am I, and look away.
She is too young to be my daughter.
I turn my eyes to the maple trees,
their colors bright and falling.
She takes the path behind my bench.
I listen for her breathing.
The trees turn in the rising breeze;
leaves whisper words of parting.
I hear the rise and fall of her,
her footfalls in the offing.
And though her sound is now long gone,
her passing voice keeps calling.

PAGE TURNER AND PIANIST

Dressed to perform,
ambition stripped
to accommodate your fingers,
I lean toward
the slow tempo of your hands
and away
as you quicken the pace,
immersed in the task,
the steady progress of form and fancy
apart from pleasures of the stave,
clinical almost, but appreciative,
leading your hands, fingers, to their place,
answering the catch in your breath,
the nod of your head
that tell me
you are ready for more…
and then touch, turn
page upon page
until the bottom sheet
is folded in place
and you are taken
at last to your final measure
beyond any need of me—

the me ambitious,
the me who wishes
nothing more
than
to shed these sheets,
this line and measure,
these notes,
your hands,
your face—
cast them all out
and then lower myself
in the round, rolling,
untended pleasure
of music.

MEMENTO MORI

Collusion in the dark
of lips on cheek and neck—
the wet, enduring kiss,
your gently arching back,
the whisper of each button drawn
through each embroidered slit,
the straps of your brassiere
sliding to your wrists;
the undertow of belly,
buttocks, thighs, and hips;
the moment fat with absent sound
as we returned to our kiss;
the hollow, clean concussion
as teeth on teeth we met—
that sound of bone on bone
recalled
after fallen cloth and flesh.

SAFE HOUSE

Hooligans are out tonight,
invited by the moon
to scamper down the drainage pipes,
scuttle through the culvert.
Their blood sings big
in the dappled dark,
each tiny heart
drunk on a winter's stone.
The stove has light enough for me,
its fuel, ally to the trees,
neatly prone, near the stove,
hewn and stacked, dried and aged, with
no sense of a self in former days.
The log shifts against the grate,
moans, as trees brush my little room,
my eave and glass, and bend low, as if to listen
for the torment of their own.
Woods without, wood within,
but creatures at the threshold
are no match for this fire-lit room.
One day, they may take me for their own,
make of me dirt and bone. Then
I too will be governed by the moon.
But not tonight. I walk across the hardwood floor
to pull the curtains closed.
Then I double latch the door.
One can never be too sure.

PORTSMOUTH, OHIO

See the sunburned peasants here
caught in the snare of icy winter;
the rain and snow, mix, enfold
the small hard homes along the river.
You see heroes on the levee walls,
Branch Rickey, Roy Rogers, soldiers, all,
who now, supine, circle
the Civil War Memorial.
The shoe factory
that once paid out
makes room for starlings now,
lost in the last and sole
of its moldering, echoing corridors.
It's Christmas in Portsmouth,
toys and sleds, empty pews,
hundred-watt crèche,
small lawn lights
of cheering descent.
You there, with the foreign face:
remember this muscled resolve,
the amazing grace
of people, place,
who know their own—
from hospital cradle
to hospice wait.

From start to finish,
we sing each name—
nuisance, neighbor,
lover, friend—
and greet each life
till the murmured end.

LIFE IS SHORT

When the guard is on the nod,
when the docent and her entourage
move on to see the Romans—
or better yet, the Dutch and the Italians—
I confess
among the Greeks
I drift to touch, caress
their marble buttocks, elbows, hips;
press my hand against
stone-enveloped ribs,
me alone, Agora of my own,
astonished at their lifeless chill.

Those Dutch girls, yes, we know,
can turn a head,
pitchers spilling,
golden lashes, slate-blue eyes,
beams a-brace against the coming night;
and Italians—
men, women,
bare chests, breasts
brimming,
the dark and light
of country stable and city sky.

Yet with the Greeks
my siren dreams abide,
and with them, so do I.
Life's lie is not with them,
I know, as with warm and wanting hands
I come, I go—
a moment's cipher in the midst
of such lovely frozen permanence.
With silent lips
they bend my ear:
Before and after,
we are here.

MY FINGERS

My fingers move in the dark of the study.
They fall and rest and rise again
from soft petals
of keys
transcribing
how I scraped back the chair
near the swimming pool edge,
promised to return
from fetching a drink
and digging for change,
saw her ringlets of hair
above the soft, tan river of cheek and neck,
followed that river as far as it went,
dove quick and deep
in her shimmering skin
and, rising for air,
saw her turn
and laugh with her friends.
That is why
these hands move in the dark of the study,
fall and rest and rise again
from soft petals
of keys
transcribing:
late-night fingers
on afternoon skin.

LEGERDEMAIN

The biologist and astronomer know
the slight, delicious
movement of a hand
that leads the eye to know.

At the bakery,
a boy
carries from the oven
a tray of conjoined rolls,
and softly,
tenderly, as if lifting an infant,
he separates the buns,
placing them on wax sheets
one upon one
upon buttered one.
He looks at me,
daring me to choose:
his soft, silent hands
or the rolls.

INFIDELITY

That certain phone booth
beneath a plate-glass sky
angles the sun
to autumnal decline.
Leaves, broken like scripture,
arraign me in ballet.
A fracture of love
drains my moments.
Home is in the mirrors.
Mirrors are in the knives.
I give you her freckled smile
and steal the loving from your eyes.

SUGARPLUM FAIRY

This is my chair—velvet, first ring, and free,
sight lines above the rake of the stage.
I know her, you see:
her morning tilted coffee,
the sound of her key,
her tumbling hair from bun to her waist,
the number of strokes her comb at night takes.
There are times, I confess,
blood warms my skin, my hands in a twist,
as she moves through those steps,
a puppet, contrived for the pleasure of men
to raise a leg, extend a hand,
convincing, with grace, but not of her senses.
It's plié, pirouette, plié, port de bras,
the grammar of cuckolds as she ascends and revolves.
When klieg lights cool and mirrored lights dim,
I wait in the shadows for her pillowed breath,
the turn of her legs, her open hips,
the tilt of her face—brow, cheeks, and neck.
She takes my hand and sweetly accepts
my clumsy bouquet. Then I am the prince.

RAIN CANNOT KNOW

Rain cannot know where it will fall—
in the graveyard, playground,
an alley between phone calls,
on shins and feet of umbrellaed lovers.

All is pursuit of wet and salt,
so the nurse will tell;
ink driven by monsoon
to find a page—
so tells the sculptor in his atelier.

Ask the motel maid gathering sheets.
She will say the same.

How are you shaped—
in tears, evening talk of lovers
circled at the waist,
oils mixing at an easel
in a sunlit place?

A nurse once told me
the sea is every place.

II

MAGRITTE

Impossible Mediterranean blue—
craggy Mallorca dust—
a woman among uniforms
deforms reason.

Locomotive clouds fill the sky,
give her sweet siren words
an utterly gifted cry.

In the market
I test her truth with mine
and find

a fish in a sky in a bucket.
Sometimes it feels so good to fly.

BARCELONA

Barcelona was the storybook:
cigars on the boulevard
and wash of perfume,
the heat of the day at the back of the neck
that took no hat for an answer.

The crowd moved as all crowds:
gathering,
order, disorder,
always the scent of blood
and threat of the maybe mob.

ORPHEUS

I hear you, Orpheus,
lamenting
not loss
but lack of resolve,
that stumbling, mendicant reflex
that turns the eye,
turns the muscle,
turns the bone
toward every veiled light
and the possibility it enfolds.

SEA CHANTEY

To a slow strum and chill drum of rain on shingles,
a wood fire dances the walls of the shed
as night and cold through chinks in the door press in.
Wife of the fisherman plaits her net.
She mends, braids line for the catch,
her fingers scented in young winter fish.
Her fisherman studies the length of his craft,
jealous eye prowling for breaks in the skin.
Odd swells tempt those rough, searching hands.
The children, in bed, take to the wet
that hammers the glistening glass—
not words of rain but a saltwater plaint,
coming, calling
next
for them.

MANET IN SEVILLE

There is a doorway,
wood of beam, wood of lintel,
that spreads
the stone and mortar wide.

There is a woman,
supple, sinewed,
dressed in shadow, eyes
wet with Gallic light.

Her shape is for the doorway,
as if the lintel, as if the beams
were canvas stretchers
and she a painting come to life.

I SHOULD HAVE KILLED YOU IN BAYONNE

I should have killed you in Bayonne—
in that languid, idle sun,
stretched against the press of grass
on the rise above the baseball path.

In that town of hands and shanks,
tinned in vinyl-sided cans,
the path they walk is regular.
Coffee steams from morning cups.
Women travel plump to fat.
Their thighs gird the kitchen stove.
Men still wear their Sunday best
each Sunday afternoon.

The sky was perfect.
Your face, perfect too.
Longing lines of cry and laugh
issued expectant from your loom.

I should have killed you in Bayonne.

TAKI 183

I heard
Taki 183,
they take old subway cars
by barge out to sea
and dump each
silver carcass,
the eviscerated seats,
knife-etched skin,
the whole tattooed beast—
yeah, all that graffiti,
Taki 183.

Just like that,
they dump them
into the sea.

So now
flounder,
bass,
jellyfish too
travel the IRT,
pause to ponder
that name
so familiar
and wonder,
in their fishy ways,

What the hell
is Taki 183?

ASTRONOMER

The sun comes first, always,
brawling, braggart, bright;
dependable, yes, but ill mannered in his likes.
The moon, to and from the sun, leans and flies,
midwife of reflected light: changing, decorous,
a consort to the night.
And you, before the windowed stars,
spin in borrowed light.
I see the rise and fall of you,
topography of desire.
How natural, then,
for me to ask and
you to lend a parcel of your light.
Not yours to give? Perhaps.
But neither yours to stem.
And if you so attempt,
I'll take with no regret.
See, already, how you ride
the convex of my lens,
the sun, the moon, and you aligned
in this instrument of delight.

CHIEF ENGINEER OF THE MS
AURELIA

In the riveted womb,
he listened to
the idea of the ocean,
the weight of a teeming saline dream
arching round
and round.

On pendulum wire
the bare bulb looped
shadows down and up the room.
Motors and gyros turned in turn;
tugboats nuzzled the waterline bow.
The *Aurelia* swung loose.

In the riveted womb,
his old bones moved
to dial the turns
of the engine room
as they parted the harbor
and parted the past—
the man and the ship and sea.

MICHIGAN

The plank board barn
stands in snowy hills.
The heater whirs in the rented dash.
That bird, flown north,
spirals past the
curve in the road
toward the barn,
at this,
the first spring melt.
Water and earth, suck and slog;
the sky whistles through
slatted walls;
brazier light
trained to the cracks
strikes the dirt barn floor,
where lifted high on four-by-fours,
blotched, discolored,
but shaped to the eye
so even blind
my hands recall
how they touched
her sweeping, unhurried curves,
rests the body of my grandfather's Ford.

The hills,
the barn,
the circling bird,
remains of a car
off a country road,
tribute offered, tribute deferred:
reasons to take the long way home.

RIVERA

Make of her a face as full
and variable as the moon,
small enough to view at once
yet so large,
without heroes and history
it cannot be viewed entire.
Perch your broad ass
on scaffold planks.
Let swing, earth to ceiling,
immense,
wonderful things.
Roll that paunchy underarm.

DOWN BESIDE THE SAN
FRANCISCO BAY

He went to San Francisco,
walked the shore,
felt sea-wet rocks
slip beneath his Oxfords,
crouched down, hunched his back
curved by all his wayward burdens,
and gathered seaweed,
ribbons of seaweed,
topped with tousled green bells and
starfish, tangled ribbons of black and green—
retrieved these from the ankle-deep water.
He put the seaweed in a box
and mailed it to me.

My father thought of me
as he walked that western shore.
I think of him, then, thinking of me,
as I remember something I have never seen,
for now he is buried in Australia.
Someday his wife will leave that place,
and with her, their daughters too.
He will be alone.

Perhaps, then, I will fly
New York to San Francisco,
stop along the shore,
gather seaweed, travel days to his foreign grave,
and mix seaweed
with the packed dry dirt of Australia.

OLD LOVE

Foolish it was
to look you up,
to find the flame of your name
in that small local paper,
a society of words, words, words,
and your photo on the page—
the happy refined living that has come,
an easy world of polish and praise
that moved toward you
as you turned its way.

I think of other things
but now and then of you,
especially while in this December plane
high, high, so implausibly high
above the rise and fall of the
white-parceled plain.
Thirty thousand feet,
the pilot interrupts to say.
Yet even from this height,
all beneath is clear, articulate
as the woven linen of this page.

So I think of you, as I did then,
the way you moved through snow
or just above,
your skis leaping to the
arc of your hips,
tracking the perfect curve
of a snow-dressed then.
The white dust in the light
swirled in your passing.
A nimbus, now, without its angel.

Through that small divide
of Plexiglas,
I lean into the wintery wind,
search the shimmering hills until
I find you
there,
down there,
out there,
somewhere in all the white,
by time, by distance
made small,
infinitesimal,
but true as this
last black speck.

SOUTH AFRICA

At customs, she asks
where I have been.
Sweat twinkles
across her broad black face.
The lamp swings
small white circles
above my luggage.
I say, "Empangeni."
She reaches for a zipper.
I'm proud of the way that Zulu name
moves easily between us.
She chuckles and calls to her friend.
"Em-pan-geni," she shouts.
And they both enjoy the Zulu sound
as she rummages through my stuff.

Two years on, an accident
of conversation returns me to that town:

"Empangeni? Yes, of course. That means
'place where stolen goods are found.'"

SOLILOQUY

Give me the language
of the mute, the deaf,
whose words have no audience,
whose audience has no words,
whose hands flutter
like butterflies
over disregarded coffee cups,
who touch so soon upon meeting—
not to absolve the risk of greeting
but to say,
Here, here, and here—
these are my gifts:
to work nouns and verbs
from pieces of the sky,
shape them to your eyes,
and watch your hands reply.

Spare me the noise
of this misbegotten jaw.
Let me speak
to you
and you to me
each time
our fingers meet,
a laying on of hands
that lends
silence to our speech.

IT CAN BE

It can be a woman, a dog,
patterns on the ceiling
in the middle of the night
that tug you toward
the weeds, the woods,
that make a path
where none had been.
The colorless leaves
grieve the creaking clapboard house.
The dog wanders room to room and
has done so for hours,
her claws clacking on the pickled pine.
I hear her
at the threshold of our room.
She too listens to the trees
and watches their shadow play
sifting through the knotted blacks and grays
waiting, with me,
for your lips to find their color
at the beginning of the day.

LAKE MICHIGAN WIND

Fat sand shivers
frozen quick
jumble the shore at dawn.
Wind slides down the dune,
knows each blade of grass,
forgets each blade of grass,
cowlicks the waves
rising to Michigan.

Low-slung clouds,
geese, and sleeping sand
ride in its invisible hand.

JUSTICE FOR ALL

I am one
to hurry down
and join the mob
at lynching time,
to stamp, guffaw,
enjoy the crowd
in a swirl of
beer, ice cream,
and fireflies.

And I
wait patient for
the freight train sound,
as boxcars
spill their prisoners out,
and eye the prettiest
of them all.

Oh, I cheer loud,
thumbs up and down
with all my friends
in the Roman crowd;
with banter, blood,
I sing along
to all my fellows' circus songs.

But I have, too,
in greater days
felt that hemp,
knelt and cried,
and begged the mob
to spare my life.

I've stumbled through
the railway yard,
the echoing ramp,
eyes cast down,
and hid my breasts
beneath a shawl.

I've known the stench
of the lion's mouth,
heard the crying
of the crowd,
and wondered at my
Lord, my love,
mercy coming in
blood and dust.

Look here, now—
a dish to wash,
tub to scrub,
another trimming of the lawn,
and a face to shave
with this mirrored one.

Shade or light?
The story old.
Stubble white.
Still, I do not know.

HEAT

The heat is here.
The dog is deaf
with her own panting.

Clouds are thick,
nearly at my knees,
pouring up the drainpipes.

Somewhere, a deck chair creaks
beneath the weight
of a businessman.

Somewhere, dark women,
faces gleaming,
parade their colors in the street.

I hear children darting
through a sprinkler;
their voices shine
like ice cubes in this heat.

CARBON COPY

My father prayed in 10-point type,
spun ribbons off their spindles,
hammered sparks in gray twilight,
knocked letters from their hinges.

Every word he rhymed between
slippery purple carbon sheets
so not just he or I would see
but all would know his splendor.

They closed the coffin at his wake,
interred him in a padded box
where now reside but replicas of
his great, still, ink-stained fingers.

III

SHETLAND ISLANDS

The wet in the wind touches her cheek
each dusk as the dories sail in
to rest in the cove of the harbor.
The soles of the boats are brimming with fish,
their dancing scent of life and death
taken ashore, a theft and a gift.
And the whitewashed walls
that brace her back
summon this man
to fire, to cups, to dishes,
to yarn she has braided
in sweaters and hats
that hang above puddles
on the floor by their bed.
And the wet of the wind
bangs door to door.
And the wet of the wind
beats on the glass.
And the peering stars
are blind to the door,
blind to the window,
blind to the sash.

A candle quivers,
brightens the back
of the coming-home man
lost in the woman,
lost in the sheets
till the whitewashed walls
fall away
in the morning
when the wet in the wind
touches his cheek
as the dories sail out
from the cove in the harbor,
to a dancing scent of life and death
of men, boats, and the Shetland waters.

NIGHT DRIVE

Headlights still the radio, wind,
deer, and moment,
feet from you and me.
We circle half this glowing hologram
until, as deer,
frame faces mute in windshield glare
caught
between a dream
and crushing speed.

HISTORY OF RELIGION

Pomegranate I was eating,
seeds and sorrow,
in a dark river
gurgling through the night.

Banana I was eating,
soft and yellow,
Latin and delicious
between my teeth.

Apple I was eating,
from a tree bent low,
pink skin filled
with tears and jubilation.

COLOR WHEEL

With light coming in,
the dog in my lap,
I think I could be
a swatch of color
in a Pierre Bonnard painting—
not an original
but many times copied,
given and taken,
a leaving and lifting of things
that came before.

With the light going out
and the dog in my lap,
I think I could be
brushes of black
in a Mark Rothko painting—
the darkness of me
to others unknown,
base, original,
and yearning

for light coming in,
a dog in my lap,
and colors to hide
and hold me.

THE SHED

Of course, I was correct.
It was a place
of promise and decay,
possibility and possibility at end.
Driving by that field,
I'd thought,
It smells like a funeral here.

Today there is a smell,
a creature trapped
inside the shed.
When winter came,
he came, too, and never left.
I know the smell:
a dog's last breath
while cradled in my lap,
an uncle lost to age and trial,
my hand pressed against his cooling head.

More telling,
I know it—
not by fields,
not by lost and parting love—
but in myself.
What is this about my hands
(what have I touched?)
(what have I tended?)
to make them seem
so unlike me in their intentions?
They do not feel funereal,
not yet. But there's a hint.

Wind whispers in the fields.
Corn lays down to rest.
Dogs stagger in waiting rooms.
Nurses draw curtains around our beds.

I lift the latch,
press the door,
and step in—
to a mute and echoing black.

LEASH LAWS

Halter of the curb and street
keep my hands from in my pockets;
tug me, sniffing, from the door
of girls arranged on twos and fours
or from leaning in my colleague's face
to bite him on the nose.
A compliant man
of bed and board,
now and then a treat or two—
shake hands, lie down, roll over, stay,
up to earn my dollar—
I walk the route of argyle socks,
dapper
in this collar.

RAFT OF THE MEDUSA

Now we only glimpse these things.
Ships of childhood
no longer take to sea.
That wide, roiling tempest
holds, buffets, sinks
no common man. Seas
no longer carry
men, women
days on end.
Oh, yes,
a boy
may entertain
a saline possibility
as he tastes the
sporting shoulder
of a friend;
or, maybe, lovers cling
in tinctured wet,
contained caress
to spend
the pittance of ambrosia
they possess;
or we who stand before
this picture in the Louvre,
free of struggle, free of care,

note the name, enjoy the framed
treachery and tumult,
read the placard,
then shuffle on
to *Winged Victory*
down the hall,
who waits to hold us
in her absent arms.

EARTH SCIENCE

Now the autumn leaves have come,
yellow, red, stubborn brown,
lanterns of a sovereign star,
Japanese garden of the heart.
On the bridge, then as now
we pause, admire the rippling rock
and koi who eye the cooling stars
and winter's cold and crippling lock.
These fortunes in the moment haunt
the leaves, the fish, though hardly us,
assured by faith in circling clocks
that scorn the seasons. Ticktock.
End, begin, round and round.
Begin, end. The clock shuts down.

A LOVING WIFE

There is a woman
curled nearby
in pleated dreams
of Noah's dove and ark.
She is comely and kind and
wears her slippers in the yard
so as not to soil her feet.

She is not the one from Leningrad
who left with scissored paintings
in her purse.
Nor the one of Saudi stars
retired to slatted blinds
and mosques.

She breathes in cadence—
a domestic drum,
prepares breakfast
after the alarm,
and when you leave,
will tidy up the house.

MY DOG, PENNY

Twelve months by the calendar,
thirteen by the moon
since I carried you last
to that fluorescent room.
By calendars
I measure my time,
but moons
were always for you.
They swelled your shadow;
your silhouette claims
on trees, houses, and roads.
Inside, there is much that is you—
the cushion that cradled your hips,
a blanket that still holds your breath,
and hairs, god knows how or from where,
that float room to room.
But moons bring me to you.
Tonight, there's a moon in the yard
climbing the porch,
one in the window,
one at the door.

I reach for the latch,
swing open the world
to light in the trees,
light on the houses,
light in the road.
Hey, Penny,
my Penny.
You ready?
Let's go.

PAINTER AND MODEL

The ashtray rattled
on the wood desk
as she stubbed out
one last cigarette.
She rose once,
finally;
flesh and bone of each preparatory sketch
moved beneath a dark-green skirt
and a sweater, ribbed black,
so that none
but his hand
could recall her
from the doorway, threshold,
shadowed carpet at the end of the stair
and the sunlight swimming beyond frosted glass.
This was her egress.

Even now, as the door
settles in its latch,
his canvas glimmers
with colors that she left.

PET

I realized
she thought of me
as if I were a cat:
distracted, errant,
pacified by
a stroke or two,
a cuddle in her lap,
marveling
at the mealtime magic
of swinging cupboard doors,
content to
romp and range
her single-bedroom flat,
charming
in my vague belief
in a world
beyond the window screen.

SHOOTING STARS

We, like Achilles, know it will end,
and when we can, we tell a story
to brighten that dark transit.
It burns young for any man,
a boy in his room, turning pages,
fingers a-play with matches.
Or a woman at her vanity,
cheeks a-blush to absent hands,
warm beyond reason—she tilts her mirrored faces.
And I, now, below this roof,
watch a windowed star shoot across the land,
teased by friction to conflagration.
The gods have their day—before, now, forever—
linger in sensation. But for all their pleasure,
even pain, it's life without abatement.

In that, just once, we win.
By our gossip and by our gospels, the gods may be amused,
but when it comes to dying, we know a thing or two.

SOUL OF THE OLD MACHINE

Here
in the concert hall,
in the silent piano,
in the hands
of the old man
moving from the wings

resides the thing,
like every other thing,
that never quite transcends
the vessel
of its being.

Still, just as early lovers,
at it once again,
summon one another
to the quick of their
bare, near-permeable skin,
so too his fingers
draw notes
from the keys,
and the keys ring
sounds around his sleeves,
cataracts

that move among us in our seats,
that make it possible to recall
the sound, the scent,
the taste, the touch of...

Inside our gray and balding skulls,
with eyes closing to the sound,
once again we recall
this is how it feels
to kiss, to touch, to love.

IN HIS IMAGE

With the pyramid
there is no quarrel
about grace, shape,
proportion, or creation.
The pharaoh's stone is squared just so:
face, shoulder, hip, torso,
each according to the code,
written and unwritten,
master to apprentice
as sun and stars, wind and moon
comb and toss the desert folds.
Pictures on a pedestal
tell who we tell ourselves
this god, this goddess was and is.
But maker of this god, this goddess:
How shall we know him?
Elbow to open hand
is the measure that he used,
a signature of sorts, his and his alone,
the rhyme and rhythm of his bones,
face, shoulder, hips, torso
repeated in the stone,
and so by his creation,
the measure of a man is known.

FADO

Music
of old lovers and old dogs,
autumn leaves, and tiled walls,
of fingers pressing guitar strings,
women singing just because
the body wants its story told
of young lovers, young dogs,
spring flowers, and whitewashed walls,
till tables clear and shutters close,
and hard black cases
are latched and stowed,
music stands swiveled down,
and all is said in the velvet dark
in words whispered, or not all—
see those strings
tremble on
the belly of the guitar.

RED SKY AT NIGHT

I give the paint
a day to dry,
watch the hull
—it glistens—
ride the air
on invisible wings
above the workshop horses.
Its wet is not
the natural wet
of water
it one day will press,
but glimmering wet,
adolescent,
a thing that knows no
lover yet.
As wet dulls dry,
the boat (and I)
lean into
the parting light.
It wants another coat.
I stir more liquid white,
rehearsal for a coming life.

The moon arrives
in casement streams
through windows,
skylights, roof and beam
in the shed
and then my house,
above my pillowed eyes,
to court the water
of this dream,
trough and crest,
fall and rise.
On air I ride
invisible wings,
to come about
in the dark-sea night.

MY PLEASURE

Prefers the rimming rhyme
of cups and spoons
to wind chimes in the random breeze;
whispered descent
of a negligee
to the fall of autumn leaves;
the rise of hands
in adoration
to blind branching of the trees.
At its best, reward greets risk
with sweetened sips, laceless hips,
and shapes to shape my fingertips.

IN MY FLORIDA

In my Florida,
there is no ocean,
just a carousel
and the Burrito King.

Yes, evening rises from Daytona
to rattle corrugated steel.
Cars corrode here.
Underbody paint is no joke.
But morning falls direct
without refracted glaze.
Seagulls never make it out this way.

So to see you on the front porch steps,
trimmed for boardwalk and the beach,
I check the horizon for a hint of damp
then reach in my pocket for the keys.

SPACE SHUTTLE *COLUMBIA*

This is how, round
a cupola cocoon
of a winter room,
snow particles travel
in tandem with the wind,
trees succumb to invisible hands
bending branch to branch,
the ground is consumed
by a press of white on black,
and verticals of place
recline beneath a white and swirling mask.

This is how, perhaps,
a drowning man
cries beneath a parting sun;
an old dog nuzzles
the hand of the man
beside the strange, metallic table;
a bird intones
evening stars have come
but this time will not last.

This is how
a particle of snow
lights,
lingers,
and melts to a tear
on the other side
of cupola glass.

ANNUNCIATION

Alone, in his chamber—
oh, monotony,
oh, jealous dream—
this god at solitaire
stretches his disembodied being,
watches the sparrow, woman, man
rise and fall and rot,
only to rise again,
all in accord with his own circling plan.
There is no beginning, no middle, no end.
No nymphs, no satyrs,
no bathing goddess and mortal glimpse—
no, at last, just a bored, dreary headmaster
with no students who comprehend.
Did he rise one day,
pack a basket—manna, wine,
a change of robes, sandals—
and then part the cloudy veil,
step to the temple's edge,
think to trek the blistering sand
to greet and visit
gods, goddesses of another land:
a place where divinity and maidens mix,
consort along riverbanks, by springs,

even, occasionally, have a fling
and make progeny to move the story
past the present rounding scheme?
From his travels, what returns did this god bring?

EPHEMERA

We know, yes, of the last man—witness to
Buddha, Moses, Jesus, or Muhammad—
the dying peasant, unremarked, in a barn,
alone among the swine and cattle,
and with him gone the final act of a new testament.
Perhaps the prophet meant little to him;
his parting thought might better have been
a debt owed, one forgiven,
rats scurrying post to post,
a mare anticipating her halter,
the moon breaking through the barn wall
to light a way for the horse's master.
And here we are, with a coming task
to recollect lost things past,
when a fellow witness no longer exists.
When you have gone—
what of, say, that childhood sled,
the bird that fell to the back porch step,
the black knit hat with the orange pom-pom,
the miscellany of all my childhood?
Your near departure already dims,
distorts these things.
When you have left, left forever,
they may stay, but not forever,
in the fading testament in my head.
I count but cannot number things
already shipped to that other place

where they stand to furnish you:
dressers, bedsteads, books, plates, and
steamer trunks, crammed for your accommodation—
but ephemera, there, they too remain,
until that day when I go too,
when we will make them whole again,
together, I and you.

ALL THAT GLITTERS

The chair is blond,
the floor, dogs too.
The woman who moves
between me and these sheets
by morning will glisten,
her curls spun gold
from the straw in this room.

All is blond; all is sun;
all is fine afternoons,
fine beyond mention,
fine beyond gloom.
I am hung in the ray
of each long afternoon,
cast by my shadow
down the drive,
down the street,
away far away,
to the dark of the east

to tunnels, to bridges,
below and above
gray city streets,
to dark weary women
whose faces I see
framed in the windows
of dovetailing trains.

Their slow bodies glimmer
with gold
on their fingers,
gold on their wrists,
gold on their necks,
and smuggled as well
between bare, jouncing breasts.
And see down the car,
that one, there,
smiling at me,
rivers of light
from her gold-capped teeth.

As I call in the dogs
and look down the street,
such is the coin
that bargains with me.

WOODLAND SKETCH

Bare bones: at once
they break and mend.
I mean by that
the branches overhead.
They have given up their color,
defiant no longer
yellow, gold, blood red,
but where there is a flutter,
grays of dwindled grieving
hang like rags in the sun.
The wind nears; empty branches rear,
and before snow's soon rise,
I find the cloven markings of a deer.
There is something about this evidence,
autumn's last descent
and winter's leaning in,
that warns the eye and ear
to the arrival of a deer.
Still, she surprises.
We each startle at the sight.
Long-lived, judging by her size—
I, too, judging by my lines—
we share a winter coloring,
wreathed in woodcut thorns.
I've come far, can claim
a provenance of place and time.

But she is here already
ten thousand years or more
perhaps to say,
in her solitude,
You are not alone.

AN OLD ORANGE BOAT

An old orange boat carried me home,
past the carillon chime of buoys
leaning with the tide
to the old beam and post
on the Staten Island side.

You can mark this trip
in quarters,
half an hour at a time,
or in years or lives.

But it's wind and water
that change the mind.
Bells, wind, and water
are the telling of the time.

ACKNOWLEDGMENTS

Many thanks to Beverly Gilmore, my mother. She has steadied my hand on deck and on land, especially in moments when I've tangled a line. I appreciate her editor's eye and many suggestions that improved this work.

I am also indebted to editor Stephanie Chou, for finding and righting the wrongs of this text, great and small. I am responsible for all the rest.

ABOUT THE AUTHOR

Richard Gilmore Loftus had a nomadic upbringing, spending time in the Midwest, Greenwich Village, Dublin, and Mallorca; in later years, finding his way to South Africa and Rwanda. He graduated from the University of Wisconsin–Madison with degrees in English literature and history, and worked in the tech and computer industries. *Dress Whites* is his first full-length collection.

Currently, Loftus lives and writes in Michigan, where he also enjoys playing piano and violin, walking with his dog, and building wooden boats.